D1030057

WELCOME TO THE U.S.A.
MASSACHUSETTS

Written by Ann Heinrichs Illustrated by Matt Kania
Content Adviser: Dr. Alan Rogers, Chair of the Department
of History, Boston College, Boston, Massachusetts

The Child's World

Published in the United States of America by The Child's World®
PO Box 326 • Chanhassen, MN 55317-0326
800-599-READ • www.childsworld.com

Photo Credits
Cover: Getty Image/Photodisc/Alanie/Life File; frontispiece: Getty Images/The Image Bank/Steve Dunwell.

Interior: Bettmann/Corbis: 13, 17; Cape Cod Potato Chips: 26; Corbis: 11 (James L. Amos), 21 (Mark E. Gibson), 23 (Ted Spiegel); Robert Deschene/Salem Witch Museum: 15; Dr. Seuss Sculpture Garden/Springfield Museums: 31; George Bush Presidential Library: 19-bottom right; Getty Images/Stone/Kindra Clineff: 6; Globe Newspaper Company: 34; Christopher P. Hamilton/In the Wild Productions: 8; John F. Kennedy Library/White House: 19-bottom left; Library of Congress: 16 (Detroit Publishing Co.), 19-top left, 19-top right; Massachusetts Office of Travel and Tourism: 18, 28; Naismith Memorial Basketball Hall of Fame: 32; George Riley/Museum of Science, Boston: 25; United States Postal Service: 30.

Acknowledgments
The Child's World®: Mary Berendes, Publishing Director

Editorial Directions, Inc.: E. Russell Primm, Editorial Director; Katie Marsico, Associate Editor; Judith Shiffer, Assistant Editor; Matt Messbarger, Editorial Assistant; Susan Hindman, Copy Editor; Melissa McDaniel, Proofreader; Peter Garnham, Matt Messbarger, Olivia Nellums, Chris Simms, Molly Symmonds, Katherine Trickle, Carl Stephen Wender, Fact Checkers; Tim Griffin/IndexServ, Indexer; Cian Loughlin O'Day, Photo Researcher and Editor

The Design Lab: Kathleen Petelinsek, Design and Page Production

Library of Congress Cataloging-in-Publication Data
Heinrichs, Ann.
  Massachusetts / written by Ann Heinrichs ; cartography and illustrations by Matt Kania.
    p. cm. — (Welcome to the U.S.A.)
  Includes index.
  ISBN 1-59296-286-6 (lib. bdg. : alk. paper) 1. Massachusetts—Juvenile literature.
2. Massachusetts—Geography—Juvenile literature. I. Kania, Matt.
II. Title. III. Series.
  F64.3.H453 2005
  974.4—dc22   2004005712

About the Author
Ann Heinrichs

Ann Heinrichs is the author of more than 100 books for children and young adults. She has also enjoyed successful careers as a children's book editor and an advertising copywriter. Ann grew up in Fort Smith, Arkansas, and lives in Chicago, Illinois.

About the Map Illustrator
Matt Kania

Matt Kania loves maps and, as a kid, dreamed of making them. In school he studied geography and cartography, and today he makes maps for a living. Matt's favorite thing about drawing maps is learning about the places they represent. Many of the maps he has created can be found in books, magazines, videos, Web sites, and public places.

On the cover: Straight Wharf is located on Nantucket.
On page one: Don't forget to stop by Boston's Quincy Market!

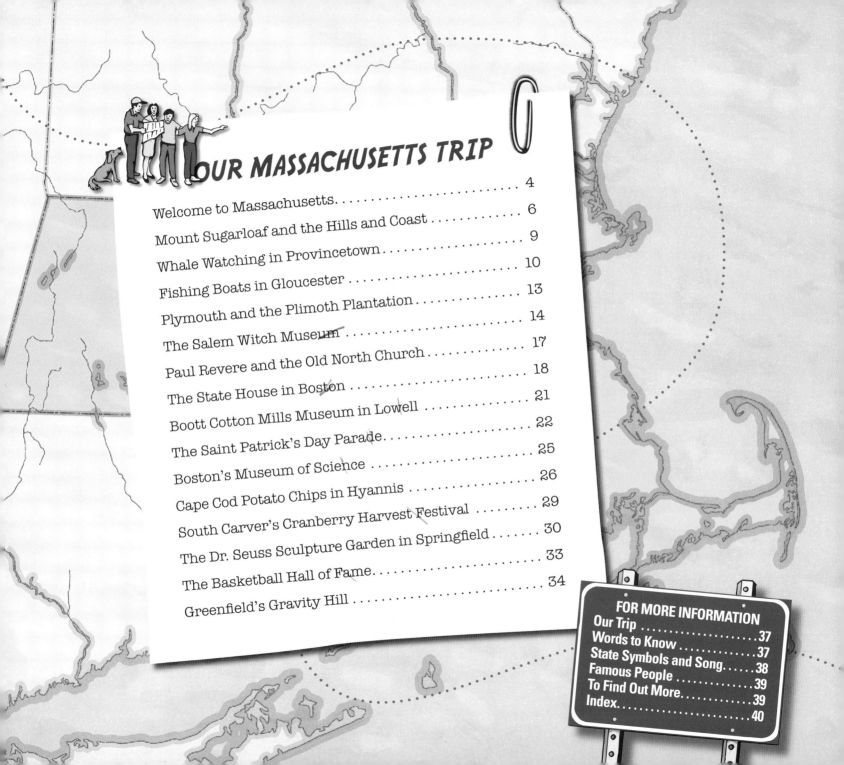

OUR MASSACHUSETTS TRIP

Welcome to Massachusetts. 4

Mount Sugarloaf and the Hills and Coast 6

Whale Watching in Provincetown 9

Fishing Boats in Gloucester 10

Plymouth and the Plimoth Plantation 13

The Salem Witch Museum 14

Paul Revere and the Old North Church 17

The State House in Boston 18

Boott Cotton Mills Museum in Lowell 21

The Saint Patrick's Day Parade. 22

Boston's Museum of Science 25

Cape Cod Potato Chips in Hyannis 26

South Carver's Cranberry Harvest Festival 29

The Dr. Seuss Sculpture Garden in Springfield 30

The Basketball Hall of Fame. 33

Greenfield's Gravity Hill 34

FOR MORE INFORMATION
Our Trip 37
Words to Know 37
State Symbols and Song. 38
Famous People 39
To Find Out More. 39
Index. 40

Massachusetts's Nicknames: The Bay State and the Old Colony State

You're in for a great tour of the Bay State! Just follow the dotted line—or else skip around. Either way, you'll have lots of fun. You'll learn some amazing things, too. You'll meet Samuel Adams and Dr. Seuss. You'll see whales and witches and parades. You'll follow Paul Revere on his midnight ride. Are you ready? Then buckle up, and let's hit the road!

WELCOME TO MASSACHUSETTS

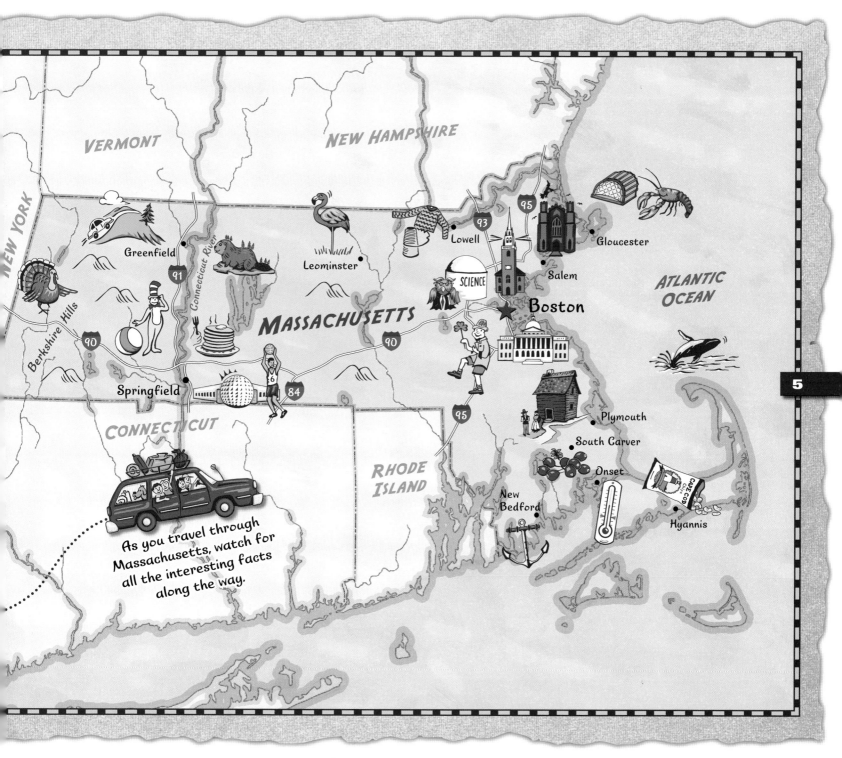

VERMONT

NEW HAMPSHIRE

NEW YORK

MASSACHUSETTS

Greenfield

Connecticut River

Leominster

Lowell

SCIENCE

Boston

Salem

Gloucester

ATLANTIC OCEAN

Berkshire Hills

Springfield

CONNECTICUT

RHODE ISLAND

Plymouth

South Carver

Onset

New Bedford

Hyannis

CAPE COD Chips

As you travel through Massachusetts, watch for all the interesting facts along the way.

Whoa, dude. That is one giant beaver! Oops. It's only Mount Sugarloaf.

Native American legends say Mount Sugarloaf is a giant beaver's body. Mount Sugarloaf is by the Connecticut River. The river runs down Massachusetts from north to south. It cuts a fertile valley through the state.

The Berkshire Hills are in western Massachusetts. Lots of snow covers the slopes in the winter.

Eastern Massachusetts faces the Atlantic Ocean. The coast is partly sandy and partly rocky. The southeast coast curls up like a fishhook. It's called Cape Cod. Lots of islands lie offshore. The biggest islands are Martha's Vineyard and Nantucket.

6

Are you a good swimmer? Many visitors enjoy the beach at Cape Cod.

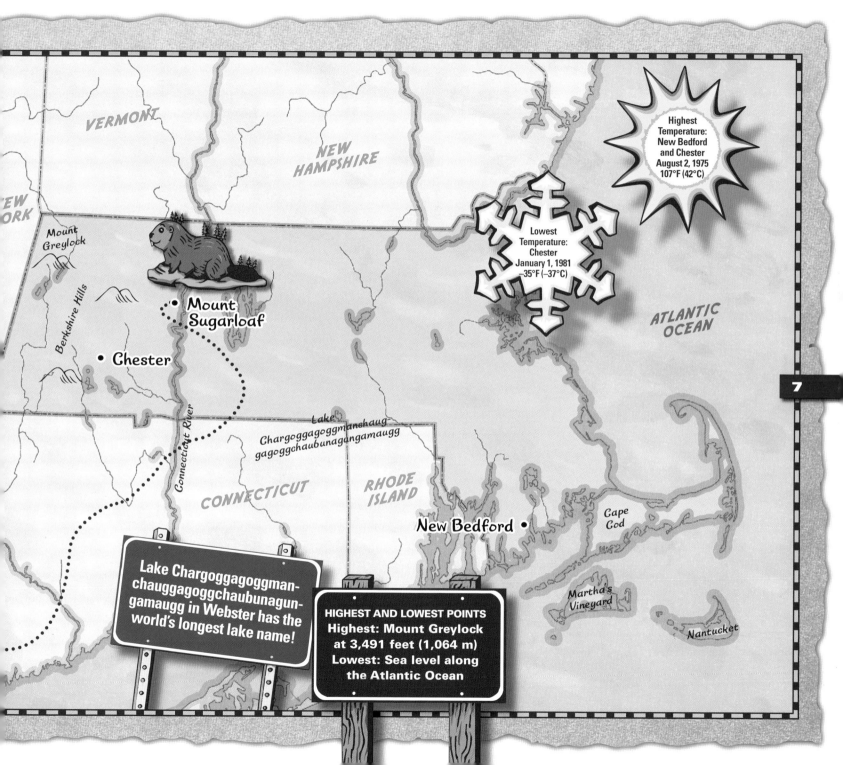

VERMONT

NEW
HAMPSHIRE

NEW
YORK

Mount
Greylock

Berkshire Hills

Mount
Sugarloaf

Chester

Connecticut River

Lake
Chargoggagoggmanchaug
gagoggchaubunagungamaugg

CONNECTICUT

RHODE
ISLAND

New Bedford

ATLANTIC
OCEAN

Cape
Cod

Martha's
Vineyard

Nantucket

Highest Temperature:
New Bedford
and Chester
August 2, 1975
107°F (42°C)

Lowest
Temperature:
Chester
January 1, 1981
−35°F (−37°C)

Lake Chargoggagoggman-
chauggagoggchaubunagun-
gamaugg in Webster has the
world's longest lake name!

HIGHEST AND LOWEST POINTS
Highest: Mount Greylock
at 3,491 feet (1,064 m)
Lowest: Sea level along
the Atlantic Ocean

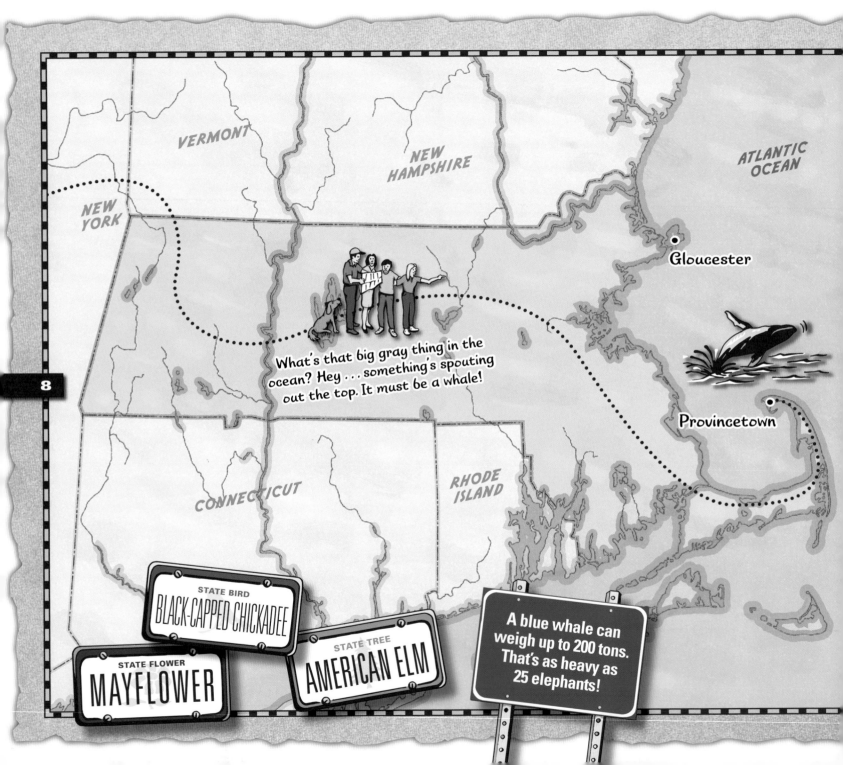

VERMONT

NEW HAMPSHIRE

NEW YORK

ATLANTIC OCEAN

Gloucester

What's that big gray thing in the ocean? Hey . . . something's spouting out the top. It must be a whale!

Provincetown

CONNECTICUT

RHODE ISLAND

STATE BIRD
BLACK-CAPPED CHICKADEE

STATE TREE
AMERICAN ELM

STATE FLOWER
MAYFLOWER

A blue whale can weigh up to 200 tons. That's as heavy as 25 elephants!

8

W ant a close-up look at some whales? Just take a whale-watching boat trip. Boats leave from Provincetown, Gloucester, and other coastal towns.

Whales, dolphins, and lots of fish swim off the coast. Lobsters and crabs live out there, too. You'll see pelicans and gulls along the shore.

Don't get splashed! You'll probably see animals up close on a whale-watching trip.

Forests cover more than half the state. Deer, foxes, and wild turkeys live there. Remember the giant beaver? Those beavers really lived in Massachusetts long ago. They were as big as bears! Today, a beaver could fit in your backpack. Now, don't get any bright ideas!

9

The National Park Service has 20 sites in Massachusetts.

This Massachusetts fisher is busy setting lobster traps.

Fishing boats are lined up in Gloucester Harbor. They catch fish and lobsters. It's fun to watch the lobster fishers. They sink wooden lobster traps into the sea. Then they come back later to collect their lobsters. How can they find their traps? They tie balloons or plastic jugs on them. These float on top of the water.

Fishing is a big business in Massachusetts. Gloucester and New Bedford are the best fishing ports. Fishers haul in cod, flounder, tuna, and other fish. Some catch shellfish such as scallops, clams, and crabs. Squid is another catch. Do you like squid? Try frying it. It tastes great!

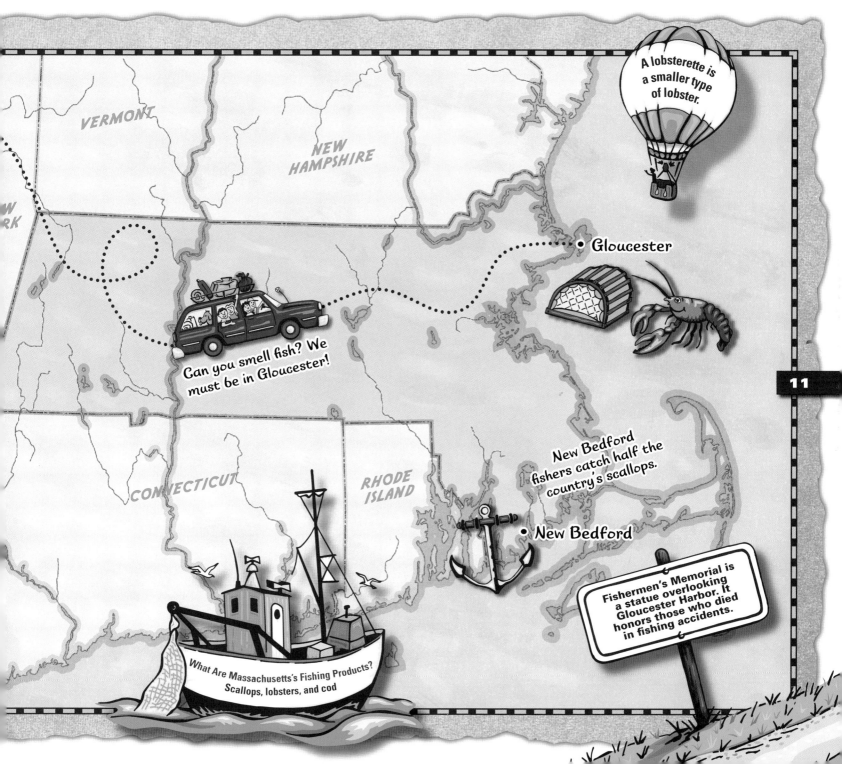

A lobsterette is a smaller type of lobster.

VERMONT

NEW HAMPSHIRE

NEW YORK

Gloucester

Can you smell fish? We must be in Gloucester!

New Bedford fishers catch half the country's scallops.

CONNECTICUT

RHODE ISLAND

New Bedford

Fishermen's Memorial is a statue overlooking Gloucester Harbor. It honors those who died in fishing accidents.

What Are Massachusetts's Fishing Products?
Scallops, lobsters, and cod

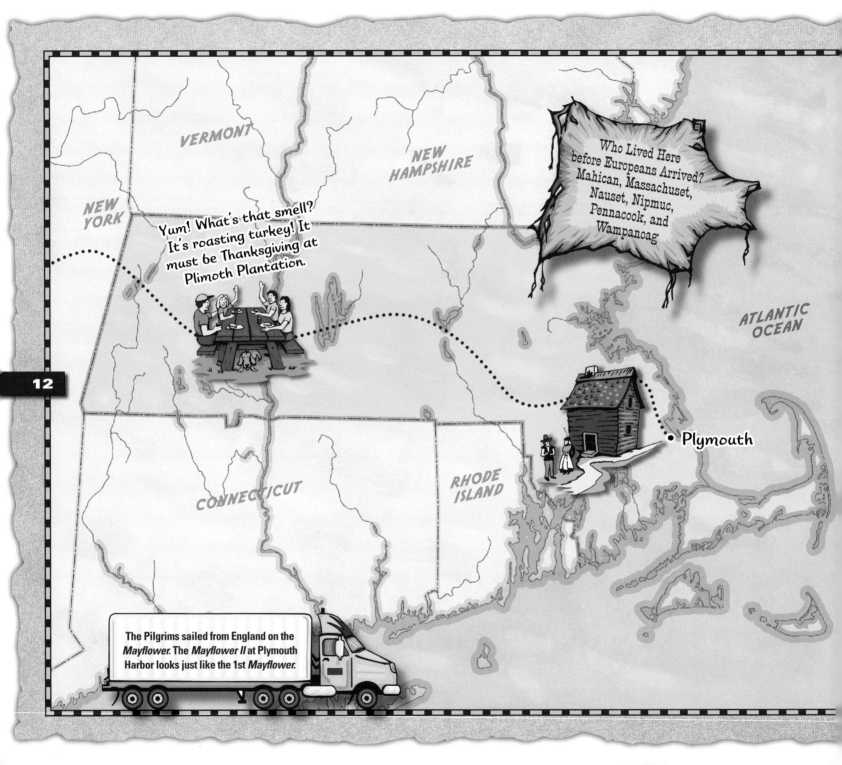

Plymouth and the Plimoth Plantation

Plymouth was the first English **settlement** in Massachusetts. (It was spelled "Plimoth" at the time.) The Pilgrims started it in 1620. They hunted and grew crops. Native Americans called the Wampanoag helped them. They all shared a big meal after the harvest. That was the first Thanksgiving.

Plimoth Plantation is a huge outdoor museum. People there speak and dress like the Pilgrims. Thanksgiving is a great time to visit. Then you can eat a big holiday meal there!

Gobble, gobble! The 1st Thanksgiving was more than 300 years ago.

England is part of Great Britain. "English" and "British" are often used to mean the same thing.

The Salem Witch Museum shows visitors what happened in 1692.

Drop by the Salem Witch Museum. You'll see lots of witches there. Don't worry—they're not real! You'll also learn about a sad part of Massachusetts history.

The town of Salem was settled by Puritans. They were a very strict religious group. They believed that witches made bad things happen.

In 1692, things went too far. Some people in Salem accused their neighbors of being witches. Many people were jailed, and nineteen were hanged. Of course, no one really was a witch.

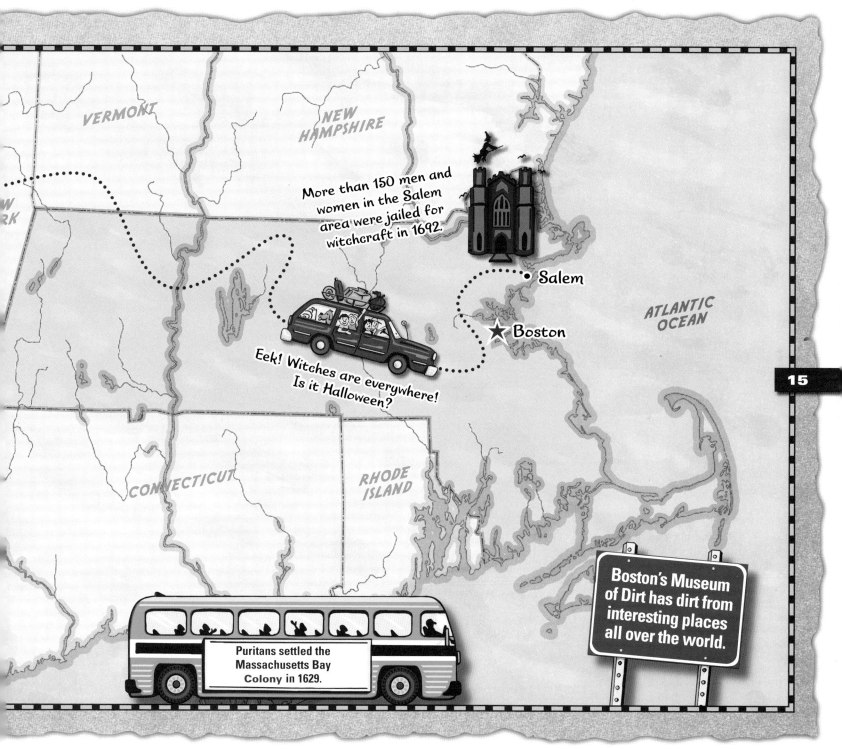

VERMONT

NEW HAMPSHIRE

NEW YORK

More than 150 men and women in the Salem area were jailed for witchcraft in 1692.

Eek! Witches are everywhere! Is it Halloween?

• Salem

★ Boston

ATLANTIC OCEAN

CONNECTICUT

RHODE ISLAND

Puritans settled the Massachusetts Bay Colony in 1629.

Boston's Museum of Dirt has dirt from interesting places all over the world.

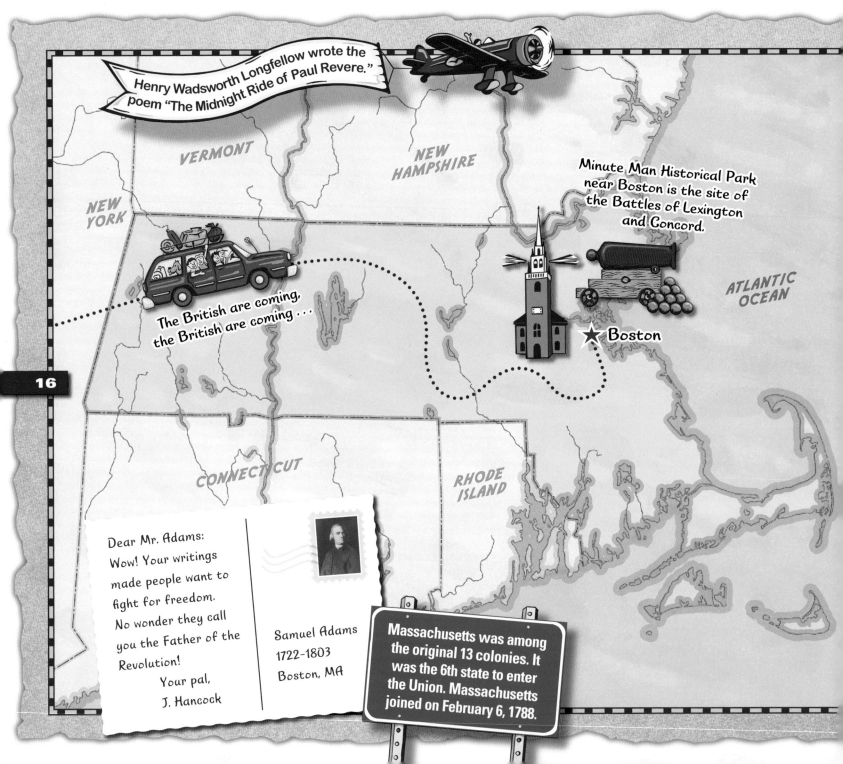

Henry Wadsworth Longfellow wrote the poem "The Midnight Ride of Paul Revere."

VERMONT

NEW HAMPSHIRE

NEW YORK

Minute Man Historical Park near Boston is the site of the Battles of Lexington and Concord.

The British are coming, the British are coming . . .

ATLANTIC OCEAN

★ Boston

CONNECTICUT

RHODE ISLAND

Dear Mr. Adams:
Wow! Your writings made people want to fight for freedom. No wonder they call you the Father of the Revolution!
Your pal,
J. Hancock

Samuel Adams
1722–1803
Boston, MA

Massachusetts was among the original 13 colonies. It was the 6th state to enter the Union. Massachusetts joined on February 6, 1788.

Paul Revere and the Old North Church

It was almost midnight. Paul Revere knew that British soldiers were coming. The colonies wanted freedom from British rule. Now Britain was sending soldiers. But were they coming over land or in boats? Revere watched the **steeple** of Boston's Old North Church. A **lookout** would hang lanterns there—"One if by land, two if by sea."

At last, Revere saw two beams of light. He had to warn people. He sprang onto his horse and dashed off into the night.

British soldiers came the very next day. They exchanged gunfire with the **colonists** in Lexington and Concord. That began the Revolutionary War (1775–1783). The colonies won. They became the United States of America.

Faster, Paul Revere! Revere made his famous ride in April 1775.

The Old North Church is a stop on Boston's Freedom Trail. Each stop is related to the fight for freedom.

Hey . . . what's that shiny thing up on the hill? It looks like gold!

The Massachusetts State House has a golden dome. You can see it glistening for miles. It's coated with a thin layer of real gold!

Inside the state house are government offices. The state government has three branches. One branch makes laws. The governor heads another branch. It carries out the laws. Courts make up the third branch. They decide if laws have been broken.

The Massachusetts State House was built in 1798.

Welcome to Boston, the capital of Massachusetts!

18

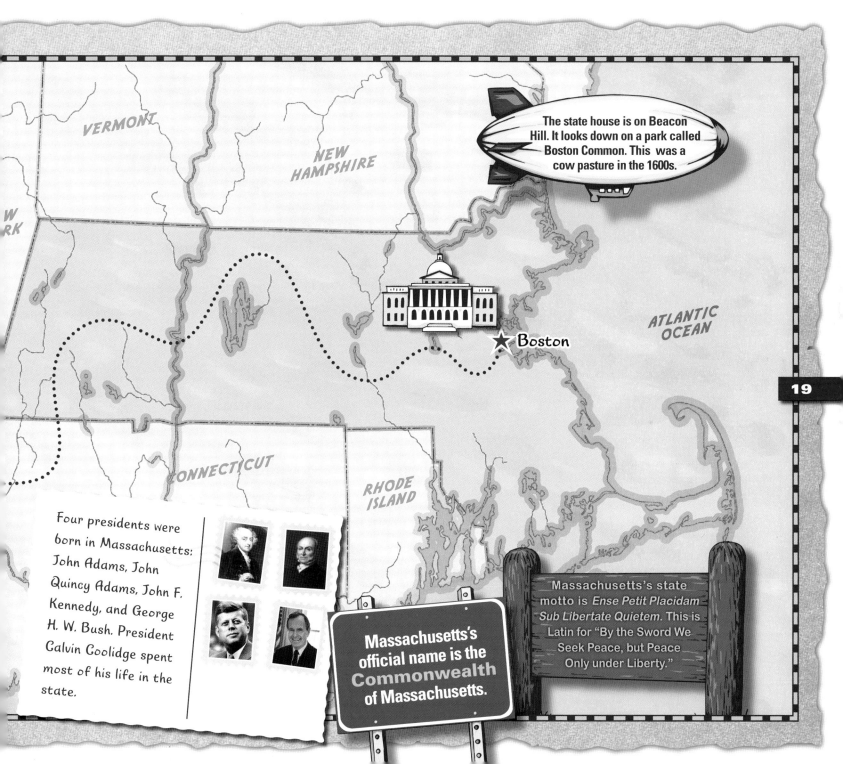

The state house is on Beacon Hill. It looks down on a park called Boston Common. This was a cow pasture in the 1600s.

VERMONT

NEW HAMPSHIRE

W RK

ATLANTIC OCEAN

★Boston

CONNECTICUT

RHODE ISLAND

Four presidents were born in Massachusetts: John Adams, John Quincy Adams, John F. Kennedy, and George H. W. Bush. President Calvin Coolidge spent most of his life in the state.

Massachusetts's official name is the **Commonwealth of Massachusetts.**

Massachusetts's state motto is *Ense Petit Placidam Sub Libertate Quietem.* This is Latin for "By the Sword We Seek Peace, but Peace Only under Liberty."

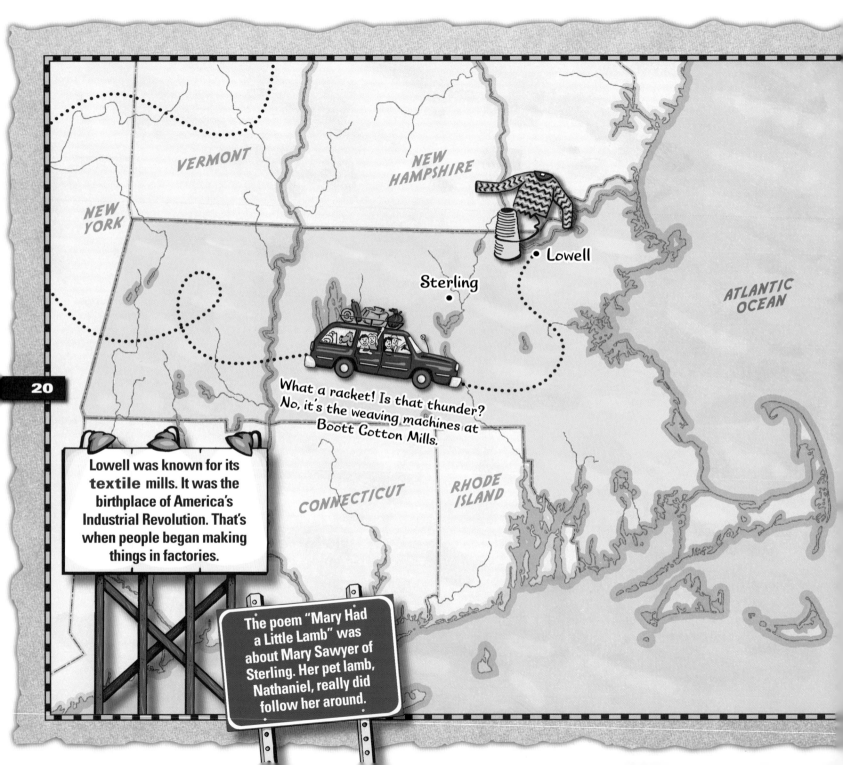

VERMONT

NEW HAMPSHIRE

NEW YORK

Lowell

Sterling

ATLANTIC OCEAN

What a racket! Is that thunder? No, it's the weaving machines at Boott Cotton Mills.

Lowell was known for its **textile** mills. It was the birthplace of America's Industrial Revolution. That's when people began making things in factories.

CONNECTICUT

RHODE ISLAND

The poem "Mary Had a Little Lamb" was about Mary Sawyer of Sterling. Her pet lamb, Nathaniel, really did follow her around.

Boott Cotton Mills Museum in Lowell

Would you make a good weaver? Visit Boott Cotton Mills and find out!

Mills were Massachusetts's first factories. They made cloth, shoes, and boots. Each mill stood beside a river. The flowing water turned a giant wheel. That made the mill's machine parts run.

Lots of **immigrants** worked at the mills. So did women and young girls. They worked long hours. The mills were noisy and dusty. Mill workers got very tired—and bored!

Check out Boott Cotton Mills Museum in Lowell. You'll learn about the people who worked there. You can try spinning and weaving cotton, too. Just put on your apron and get to work!

Look! Everybody's wearing green. Bands are marching down the street. What's going on?

The Saint Patrick's Day Parade

It's the Saint Patrick's Day parade! Boston has a big parade for Saint Patrick's Day, March 17. That's because so many Bay Staters have Irish roots. Saint Patrick is the patron saint of Ireland. Why wear green on Saint Patrick's Day? Because the shamrock, or three-leaf clover, is green. That's Ireland's national plant.

Lots of other Bay Staters are Italian or French-Canadian. Their grandparents might have worked in the mills. But that's just part of the picture. Bay Staters are like a big patchwork quilt. Their **ancestors** came from dozens of different countries!

Is green your favorite color? Don't miss Boston's Saint Patrick's Day parade.

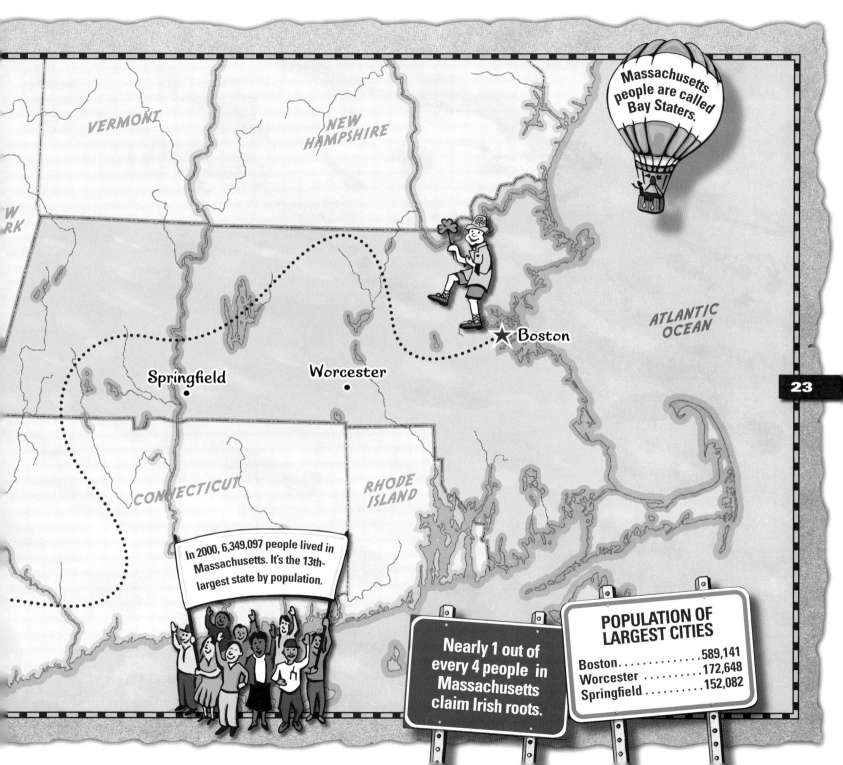

Massachusetts people are called Bay Staters.

VERMONT

NEW HAMPSHIRE

NEW YORK

ATLANTIC OCEAN

★Boston

Springfield

Worcester

CONNECTICUT

RHODE ISLAND

In 2000, 6,349,097 people lived in Massachusetts. It's the 13th-largest state by population.

Nearly 1 out of every 4 people in Massachusetts claim Irish roots.

POPULATION OF LARGEST CITIES

Boston 589,141
Worcester 172,648
Springfield 152,082

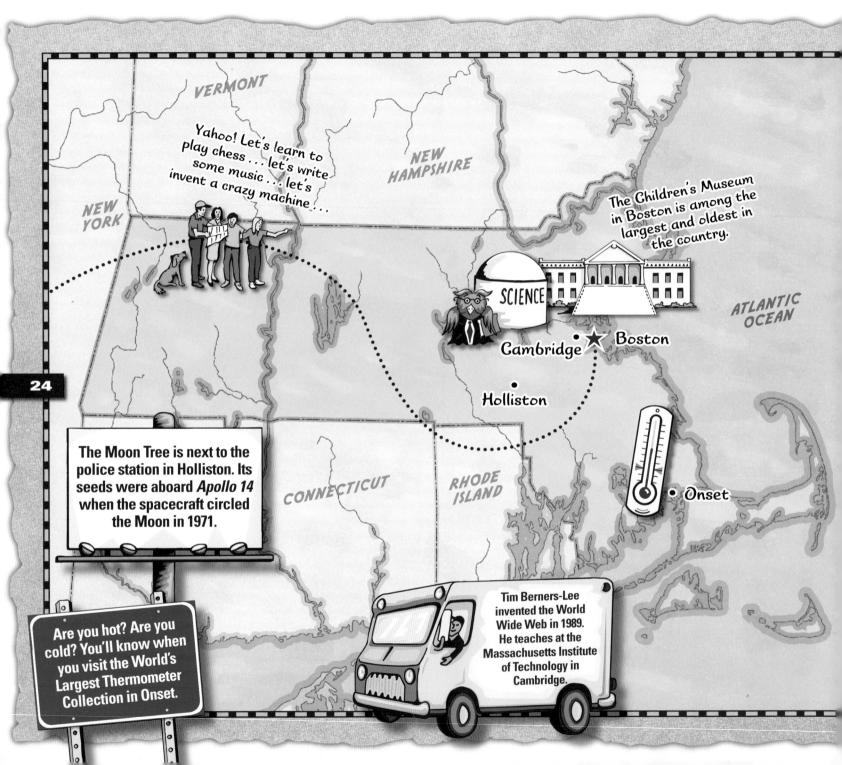

Yahoo! Let's learn to play chess . . . let's write some music . . . let's invent a crazy machine . . .

VERMONT

NEW HAMPSHIRE

NEW YORK

The Children's Museum in Boston is among the largest and oldest in the country.

SCIENCE

Cambridge ★ Boston

ATLANTIC OCEAN

Holliston

The Moon Tree is next to the police station in Holliston. Its seeds were aboard *Apollo 14* when the spacecraft circled the Moon in 1971.

CONNECTICUT

RHODE ISLAND

Onset

Are you hot? Are you cold? You'll know when you visit the World's Largest Thermometer Collection in Onset.

Tim Berners-Lee invented the World Wide Web in 1989. He teaches at the Massachusetts Institute of Technology in Cambridge.

Boston's Museum of Science

Cahners ComputerPlace is a great place to visit. It's in Boston's Museum of Science. Try out some of its computer programs. You'll learn new languages. You'll build and invent and create things. Do you like math and science games? There are plenty of those, too.

At Cahners ComputerPlace, kids play games and create crazy inventions.

Computers and science are important in Massachusetts. The mills were slowing down by the 1950s. Luckily, Massachusetts had lots of smart scientists. Some designed rockets and spacecraft. Others worked on computers. They opened up many new **industries.**

The 1st computer "bug" was a moth that flew into Mark I in the 1940s. Mark I was an early computer at Harvard University in Cambridge.

Cape Cod Potato Chips in Hyannis

Crunch, crunch. Gobble, gobble. Let's all talk with our mouths full of potato chips!

Cape Cod Potato Chips are made in Hyannis. You can tour the potato chip factory. It makes 150,000 bags of crunchy snacks every day! You'll see machines peel and slice potatoes. Then the slices are fried till they're nice and crispy.

And you get free potato chips, too. Just don't talk with your mouth full!

At first, Massachusetts's factories made cloth and shoes. Now the state's factories make lots of things. You can't eat them all. But you probably use them. They include tools, computers, and medicines.

Want a salty snack? Just stop by the Cape Cod Potato Chips factory.

Ruth Wakefield of Whitman invented chocolate chip cookies in the 1930s.

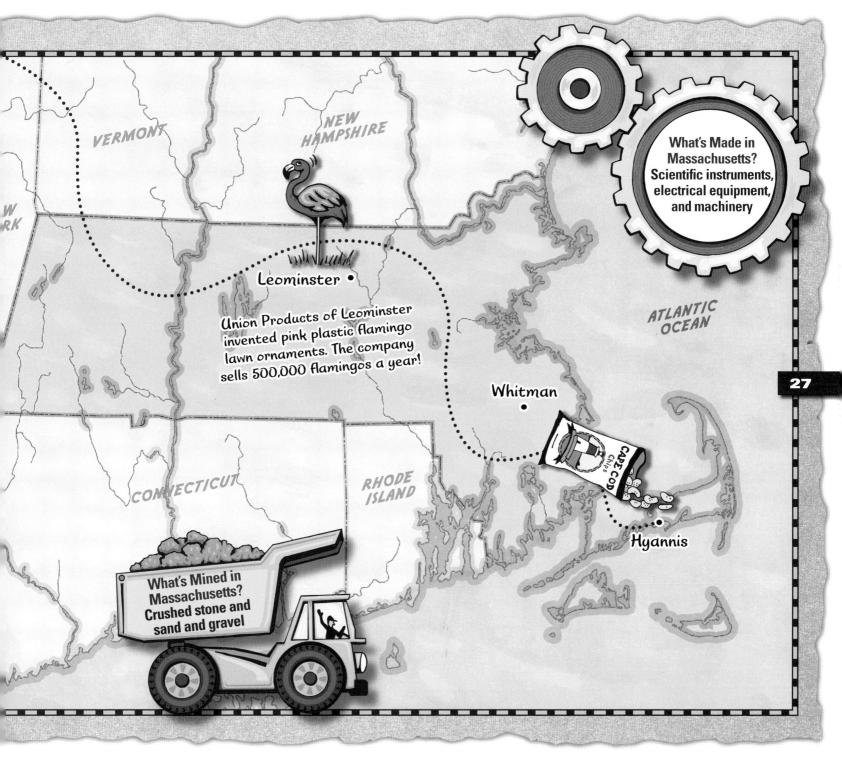

VERMONT

NEW HAMPSHIRE

NEW YORK

ATLANTIC OCEAN

Leominster •

Union Products of Leominster invented pink plastic flamingo lawn ornaments. The company sells 500,000 flamingos a year!

Whitman •

CONNECTICUT

RHODE ISLAND

Hyannis •

CAPE COD Chips

What's Made in Massachusetts? Scientific instruments, electrical equipment, and machinery

What's Mined in Massachusetts? Crushed stone and sand and gravel

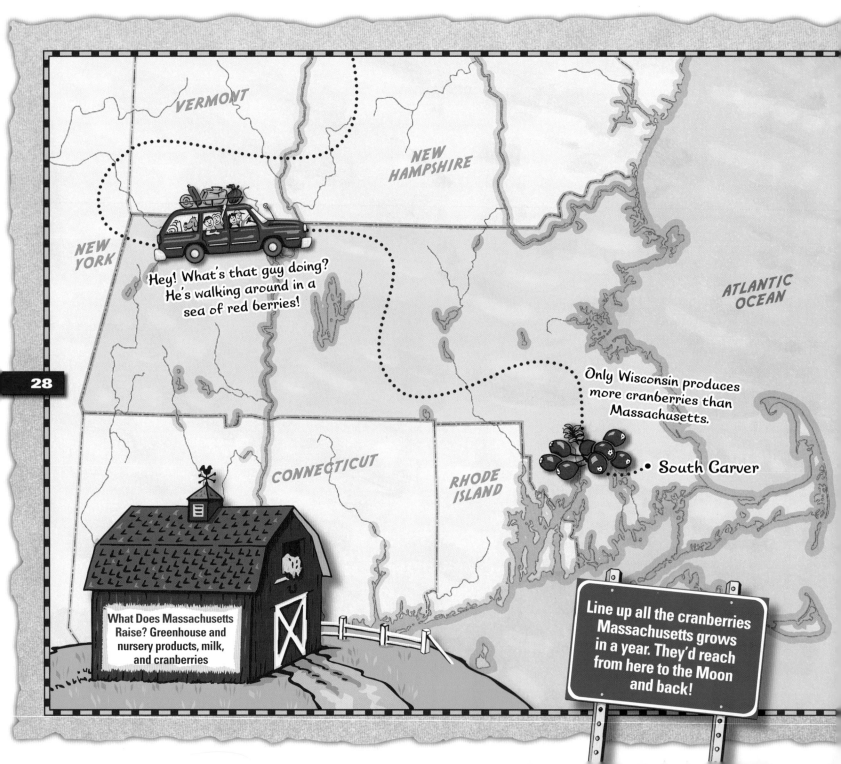

South Carver's Cranberry Harvest Festival

Cranberries are an important crop in Massachusetts. They grow in wet soil called bogs. The bogs are flooded with water at harvest time. Then the cranberries float to the top!

South Carver has a Cranberry Harvest Festival in October. You can ride a train through the bog. Don't fall in!

Many Massachusetts farmers grow flowers and bushes. People buy them for their homes and yards. Dairy farmers raise cows for their milk. They sell the milk to many other states. Some milk is used to make milk chocolate. Want a real taste treat? Dip those cranberries in milk chocolate!

Massachusetts farmers harvest their cranberry crop. These berries might be used for your morning juice!

This statue of Dr. Seuss is in Springfield. Residents are proud that he was born there.

The Dr. Seuss Sculpture Garden is in Springfield. It's got more than a dozen life-size Dr. Seuss figures. Dr. Seuss was born in Springfield. His real name was Theodor Seuss Geisel. He used Springfield streets, parks, and people in his books!

Lots of other famous writers lived in Massachusetts. They include Louisa May Alcott and Edgar Allan Poe. Nathaniel Hawthorne was born in Salem. Many of his stories take place in Massachusetts.

Henry Wadsworth Longfellow and Emily Dickinson wrote poetry. Herman Melville sailed on ships from Massachusetts ports. He wrote *Moby Dick*. It's a story about a gigantic white whale.

Harvard University in Cambridge was founded in 1636. It was the country's 1st college.

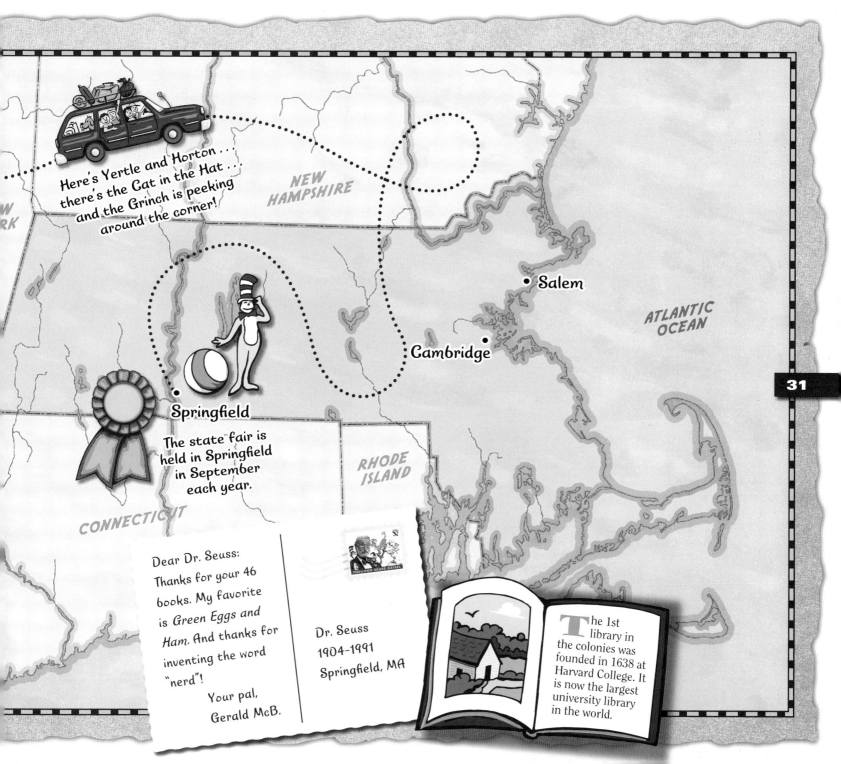

Here's Yertle and Horton... there's the Cat in the Hat... and the Grinch is peeking around the corner!

NEW HAMPSHIRE

NEW YORK

• Salem

ATLANTIC OCEAN

Cambridge

• Springfield

The state fair is held in Springfield in September each year.

RHODE ISLAND

CONNECTICUT

Dear Dr. Seuss:
Thanks for your 46 books. My favorite is Green Eggs and Ham. And thanks for inventing the word "nerd"!

Your pal,
Gerald McB.

Dr. Seuss
1904–1991
Springfield, MA

The 1st library in the colonies was founded in 1638 at Harvard College. It is now the largest university library in the world.

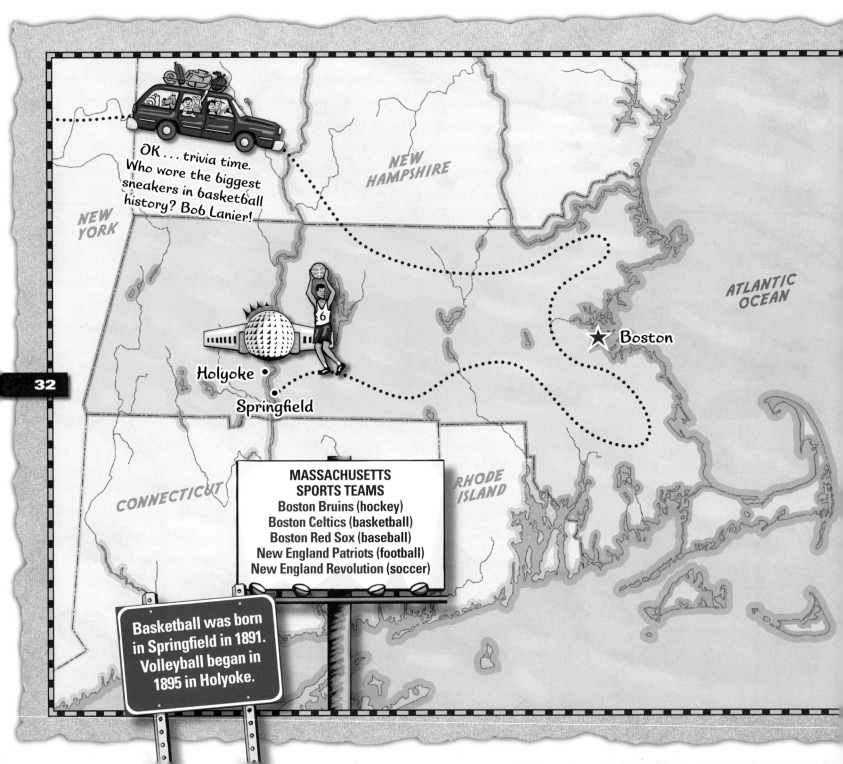

OK . . . trivia time. Who wore the biggest sneakers in basketball history? Bob Lanier!

NEW HAMPSHIRE

NEW YORK

ATLANTIC OCEAN

★ Boston

Holyoke

Springfield

CONNECTICUT

RHODE ISLAND

MASSACHUSETTS SPORTS TEAMS
Boston Bruins (hockey)
Boston Celtics (basketball)
Boston Red Sox (baseball)
New England Patriots (football)
New England Revolution (soccer)

Basketball was born in Springfield in 1891. Volleyball began in 1895 in Holyoke.

The Basketball Hall of Fame

The National Basketball Hall of Fame is in Springfield.

Want to see Bob Lanier's basketball sneakers? They were a whopping size twenty-two! Just visit the Basketball Hall of Fame in Springfield. You'll see lots of other basketball stuff there.

Bay Staters are wild about sports. Their own basketball team is the Boston Celtics. Massachusetts has four other **professional** teams. They play baseball, football, hockey, and soccer.

You can have plenty of fun in the Bay State. Just head for the coast. It's great for swimming, fishing, and boating.

In the winter, people ski down the snowy mountains. Are you a scaredy-cat on skis? Don't worry. There are lots of bunny hills for you!

Boston's Fenway Park opened in 1912. It's America's oldest baseball park.

Wait! What's going on? The car is rolling uphill—all by itself!

Suppose an apple falls off a tree. It rolls downhill, right? Not on Gravity Hill!

Gravity Hill is a spooky place in Greenfield. People swear that things roll uphill there. So what's going on? Some people say the land is really sloping downhill. It just *looks* like it's uphill. Others say ghosts are pushing the cars. Scientists are trying to figure out this mystery. Meanwhile, got any ideas?

Which way are you moving on spooky Gravity Hill?

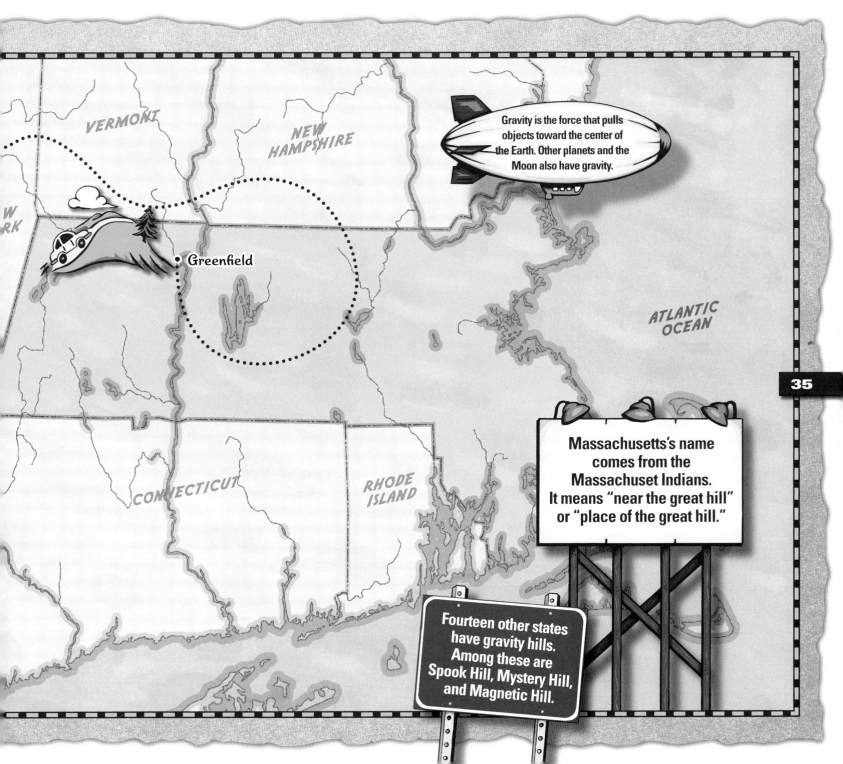

Gravity is the force that pulls objects toward the center of the Earth. Other planets and the Moon also have gravity.

VERMONT

NEW HAMPSHIRE

• Greenfield

ATLANTIC OCEAN

CONNECTICUT

RHODE ISLAND

Massachusetts's name comes from the Massachuset Indians. It means "near the great hill" or "place of the great hill."

Fourteen other states have gravity hills. Among these are Spook Hill, Mystery Hill, and Magnetic Hill.

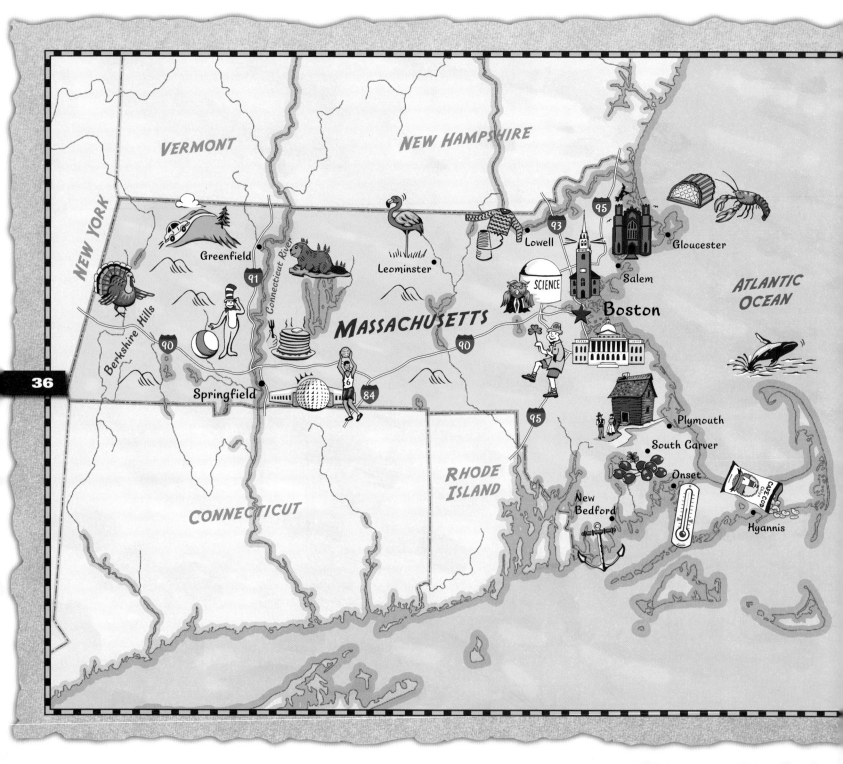

VERMONT

NEW HAMPSHIRE

NEW YORK

Greenfield

Leominster

Lowell

Salem

Gloucester

ATLANTIC OCEAN

Connecticut River

SCIENCE

Boston

MASSACHUSETTS

Berkshire Hills

Springfield

RHODE ISLAND

Plymouth

South Carver

Onset

New Bedford

Hyannis

CONNECTICUT

36

91

90

84

95

93

95

90

6

CAPE COD

OUR TRIP

We visited many amazing places on our trip! We also met a lot of interesting people along the way. Look at the map on the left. Use your finger to trace all the places we have been.

Do you remember what the world's longest lake name is? Can you spell it? See page 7 for the answer.

How much does a blue whale weigh? How many elephants is that? Page 8 has the answer.

What is a lobsterette? See page 11 for the answer.

What was the name of the Pilgrims' ship? Look on page 12 for the answer.

Who wrote a poem about Paul Revere's famous ride? Page 16 has the answer.

What is the state capital? Turn to page 18 for the answer.

Where is the world's largest thermometer collection? It is on page 24!

What are the names of Massachusetts's 5 professional sports teams? Turn to page 32 for the answer.

That was a great trip! We have traveled all over Massachusetts! There are a few places that we didn't have time for, though. Next time, we plan to have breakfast in Springfield. That's where the World's Largest Pancake Breakfast is held every May. More than 75,000 pancakes are served at this event.

More Places to Visit in Massachusetts

WORDS TO KNOW

ancestors (AN-cess-turz) family members who lived long ago

colonists (KOL-uh-nists) people who settle a new land for their country

colony (KOL-uh-nee) land that has been settled by people from another country and that is ruled by that country

commonwealth (KOM-uhn-welth) a government for the good of all its people

immigrants (IM-uh-gruhnts) people who move from their home country to another country

industries (IN-duh-streez) types of business

lookout (LOOK-out) a person who watches for something

professional (pruh-FESH-uh-nuhl) doing an activity for pay

settlement (SET-uhl-muhnt) a new land with ties to a parent country

steeple (STEE-puhl) a tall, pointy tower on a church

textile (TEK-stile) cloth

Massachusetts covers 7,840 square miles (20,306 sq km). It's the 46th-largest state in size.

STATE SYMBOLS

State berry: Cranberry

State beverage: Cranberry juice

State bird: Chickadee

State building rock and monument stone: Granite

State cat: Tabby cat

State ceremonial march: "The Road to Boston"

State cookie: Chocolate chip cookie

State dessert: Boston cream pie

State dog: Boston terrier

State explorer rock: Dighton rock

State fish: Cod

State flower: Mayflower

State folk dance: Square dancing

State folk song: "Massachusetts" by Arlo Guthrie

State fossil: Dinosaur tracks

State game bird: Wild turkey

State gem: Rhodonite

State historical rock: Plymouth Rock

State horse: Morgan horse

State insect: Ladybug

State marine mammal: Right whale

State mineral: Babingtonite

State muffin: Corn muffin

State rock: Roxbury puddingstone

State soil: Paxton soil series

State tree: American elm

State flag

State seal

STATE SONG

"All Hail to Massachusetts"

Words and music by Arthur Marsh

All hail to Massachusetts, the land of the free and the brave!
For Bunker Hill and Charlestown, and flag we love to wave;
For Lexington and Concord, and the shot heard 'round the world;
All hail to Massachusetts, we'll keep her flag unfurled.
She stands upright for freedom's light that shines from sea to sea;
All hail to Massachusetts! Our country 'tis of thee!

All hail to grand old Bay State, the home of the bean and the cod,
Where pilgrims found a landing and gave their thanks to God.
A land of opportunity in the good old U.S.A.
Where men live long and prosper, and people come to stay.
Don't sell her short but learn to court her industry and stride;
All hail to grand old Bay State! The land of pilgrim's pride!

All hail to Massachusetts, renowned in the Hall of Fame!
How proudly wave her banners emblazoned with her name!
In unity and brotherhood, sons and daughters go hand in hand;
All hail to Massachusetts, there is no finer land!
It's M-A-S-S-A-C-H-U-S-E-T-T-S.
All hail to Massachusetts! All hail! All hail! All hail!

FAMOUS PEOPLE

Adams, John (1735–1826), 2nd U.S. president

Adams, John Quincy (1767–1848), 6th U.S. president

Adams, Samuel (1722–1803), politician during the American Revolution

Alcott, Louisa May (1832–1888), author

Anthony, Susan B. (1820–1906), reformer

Attucks, Crispus (1723–1770), patriot during the American Revolution

Bernstein, Leonard (1918–1990), composer and conductor

Bradford, William (1590–1657), Pilgrim leader

Bush, George H. W. (1924–), 41st U.S. president

Davis, Bette (1908–1989), actor

Dickinson, Emily (1830–1886), poet

Geisel, Theodor Seuss (1904–1991), children's author

Hankcock, John (1737–1793), 1st signer of the Declaration of Independence

Kennedy, John F. (1917–1963), 35th U.S. president

Lyon, Mary (1797–1849), educator and founder of the 1st U.S. woman's college

Poe, Edgar Allan (1809–1849), author

Revere, Paul (1735–1818), silversmith and patriot during the American Revolution

Samoset (ca. 1590–ca. 1653), American Indian leader and friend of the Pilgrims

Squanto (1585–ca. 1622) American Indian interpreter for the Pilgrims

TO FIND OUT MORE

At the Library
Fritz, Jean, and Trina Schart Hyman (illustrator). *Why Don't You Get a Horse, Sam Adams?* New York: Coward, McCann & Geoghegan, 1974.

Metaxas, Eric, and Shannon Stirnweis (illustrator). *Squanto and the Miracle of Thanksgiving.* Nashville: Tommy Nelson, 1999.

Raven, Margot Theis. *M Is for Mayflower: A Massachusetts Alphabet.* Chelsea, Mich.: Sleeping Bear Press, 2002.

Winter, Jeanette, and Emily Dickinson. *Emily Dickinson's Letters to the World.* New York: Frances Foster Books, 2002.

Zschock, Martha, and Heather Zschock (illustrator). *Journey around Boston from A to Z.* Beverly, Mass.: Commonwealth Editions, 2001.

On the Web
Visit our home page for lots of links about Massachusetts: *http://www.childsworld.com/links*

Note to Parents, Teachers, and Librarians: We routinely verify our Web links to make sure they are safe, active sites—so encourage your readers to check them out!

Places to Visit or Contact
Massachusetts Historical Society
1154 Boylston Street
Boston, MA 02215
617/536-1608
For more information about the history of Massachusetts

Massachusetts Office of Travel and Tourism
10 Park Plaza, Suite 4510
Boston, MA 02116
617/973-8500
For more information about traveling in Massachusetts

INDEX

Adams, John, 19, *19*
Adams, John Quincy, 19, *19*
Adams, Samuel, 16, *16*
Alcott, Louisa May, 30
American Indians, 6, 13, *13,* 35
ancestors, 22
animals, 9
Apollo 14 spacecraft, 24

basketball, 32, 33
Basketball Hall of Fame, 33, *33*
Berkshire Hills, 6
blue whales, 8
bogs, 29, *29*
Boott Cotton Mills, 21, *21*
Boston, 15, 17, 18, 22, 23, 25, 32, 33
Boston Bruins, 32
Boston Celtics, 32, 33
Boston Red Sox, 32
Bush, George H. W., 19, *19*

Cahners ComputerPlace, 25, *25*
Cape Cod, 6, *6*
Cape Cod Potato Chips factory, 26, *26*
climate, 6–7
coast, 6, 9, 33
colonies, 16, 17

computers, 25
Concord, 17
Connecticut River, 6
Coolidge, Calvin, 19
cranberries, 28, 29, *29*
Cranberry Harvest Festival, 29

dairy farming, 29
Dr. Seuss, 30, *30,* 31
Dr. Seuss Sculpture Garden, 30

electronics, 25

factories, 20, 21, 26
farming, 28, 29, *29*
Fenway Park, 33
Fishermen's Memorial, 11
fishing, 10, *10,* 11,
Freedom Trail, 17

Geisel, Theodor Seuss, 30
Gloucester, 10
Gloucester Harbor, 10, 11
gravity hills, 34, 35
Gravity Hill, 34, *34*
Great Britain, 13, 17

Harvard University, 25, 30
Holliston, 24
Hyannis, 26

Industrial Revolution, 20
industry, 10, 11, 20–21, 25, 26, 28–29
islands, 6

Kennedy, John F., 19, *19*

Lake Chargoggagoggmanch-auggagoggchaubunagung-amaugg, 7
landforms, 6–7, 17, 18–19
landmarks, 6, 17, 18–19
Lanier, Bob, 33
Leominster, 27
Lexington, 17
lobster, 10
Lowell, 20, 21

major cities, 15, 15–19, 22–23, 24–25, 30, 32, 33
Mark I computer, 25
Martha's Vineyard, 6
"Mary Had a Little Lamb" (poem), 20
Massachusetts State House, 18, *18*
Melville, Herman, 30
mills, 20, 21, *21,* 25
Moby Dick (Herman Melville), 30
Moon Tree, 24
motto, 19

Mount Greylock, 7
Mount Sugarloaf, 6
Museum of Dirt, 15
Museum of Science, 25

name, 19, 35
Nantucket, 6
national parks, 9
Native Americans, 6, 13, *13,* 35
natural resources, 9, 10, 27, 30
New Bedford, 10, 11
New England Patriots, 32
New England Revolution, 32

Old North Church, 17
Onset, 24

places of interest, 6–7, 9, 11, 12–13, 14–15, 16–17, 18–19, 21, 22–23, 24–25, 26–27, 29, 30, 32, 33, 34
Plimoth Plantation, 13
Plymouth, 13
Poe, Edgar Allan, 30
population, 22
Pilgrims, 13, *13*
Puritans, 14

Revere, Paul, 17, *17*
Revolutionary War, 16, 17

Saint Patrick's Day parade, 22, *22*
Salem, 14
Salem Witch Museum, 14, *14*
science, 25
settlements, 13
shamrock, 22
shellfish, 10
skiing, 33
South Carver, 29
sports, 32, 33
Springfield, 23, 30, 32, 33
squid, 10
state bird, 8
statehood, 16
state flower, 8
state motto, 18
state nicknames, 4
state tree, 8
Sterling, 20

textile mills, 20–21
Thanksgiving, 13, *13*

Union Products, 27

Wakefield, Ruth, 26
whales, 8, 9, *9,* 30
whale watching, *8,* 9
witches, 14
Worcester, 23
World's Largest Thermometer Collection, 24

*Bye, Bay State.
We had a great time.
We'll come back soon!*